Download your free app to see the ghosts in this book. Search for *Horrible Hauntings* on the Apple App Store or through Google Play, or use this QR code. With your app loaded, interact with the ghosts by moving your view, using touch controls, or even speaking!

An Augmented Reality Collection of Ghosts and Ghouls

Horrible Hauntings

By Shirin Yim Bridges
Illustrated by William Maughan

goosebottombooks

To those who made this possible ~ **Shirin Yim Bridges**
For my grandchildren ~ **William Maughan**

Author **Shirin Yim Bridges**
Illustrator **William Maughan**
Augmented reality **Jason Yim and Trigger Global**
Book design **David Bloom**
Copy editor **Jennifer Fry**

Typeset in Be Safe, Garamond, and Volkswagen
Illustrations rendered in oil paint

Manufactured in Malaysia

Library of Congress PCN: 2012932372

ISBN: 978-1-937463-99-1

First Edition 10 9 8 7 6 5 4 3 2 1

Goosebottom Books LLC
710 Portofino Lane, Foster City, CA 94404

www.goosebottombooks.com

Featuring:

The Flying Dutchman

Abraham Lincoln

The Princes in the Tower

Whalley Abbey

The Brown Lady

The Headless Horseman

The Haunted Gallery

The Amherst Poltergeist

The Black Dogs

Bloody Mary

The Flying Dutchman

Bernard Fokke

Clinging to the top of the mast in the roar of the storm, he felt the ship buck beneath him like a stallion. The deck—far below—seemed to lurch even further away. Inky black clouds flashed with lightning. One flash, he thought, was lasting unusually long. Then the realization gripped him. The eerie light was not fading. Now, silhouetted against it, he could see the skeleton of a ship. With the fury of the gale tearing through its ghostly rigging, the Flying Dutchman was sailing straight for him.

THE FLYING DUTCHMAN is a harbinger of doom in both legend and literature. According to some, the phantom ship once belonged to a Captain Bernard Fokke. Fokke completed his trading voyages with such remarkable speed that it was rumored he had sold his soul to the Devil. When his ship disappeared mid-voyage, many believed he had simply been called to his master. In other lore, the captain of the cursed ship lost both ship and soul to the Devil in a game of dice; or doomed the ship when he defied Satan.

But the spookiest fact about the Flying Dutchman is that it's been seen repeatedly, and by many witnesses at once. On January 26, 1923, at fifteen minutes past midnight, an officer on an English ship heading for Australia reported, *"There was a strange light on the port bow…Looked at the light through binoculars and…made out what appeared to be the hull of a* sailing ship, luminous, with two distinct masts carrying bare yards, also luminous…when she was about a half-mile of us she suddenly disappeared."* There were four witnesses to the spectacle.

Even more people witnessed an encounter documented by the future King George V of England. On July 11, 1881, while serving as a seaman on the HMS Bacchante, he recorded in his diary, *"At 4 a.m. the Flying Dutchman crossed our bows. A strange red light as of a phantom ship all aglow, in the midst of which light the masts, spars, and sails of a brig 200 yards distant stood out in strong relief…"*

True to its reputation as a bad omen, tragedy followed the sighting. Later that morning, the very same sailor who had first spotted the phantom ship fell from the top of a mast and was *"smashed to atoms."*

King George V

Abraham Lincoln

As she watched, the outlines of a tall, thin man materialized next to the window. Moonlight picked out his features: a brow lined with worry; lips that were grim, compressed. Condensing slowly, as if out of sadness, the ghost of President Abraham Lincoln gazed mournfully out across the Potomac River and through time.

Abraham Lincoln

ABRAHAM LINCOLN, the legendary sixteenth President of the United States, is associated with many hauntings. He died a violent death—shot through the back of the head by assassin John Wilkes Booth while watching a play at Ford's Theatre on April 14, 1865.

Eerily, just ten days before, the president had a premonition:

> *"…I heard subdued sobs, as if a number of people were weeping…I went from room to room… Before me was a catafalque, on which rested a corpse…'Who is dead in the White House?' I demanded of one of the soldiers. 'The President' was his answer…"*

A train draped all in black carried Lincoln's body back to his hometown of Springfield, Illinois. Millions turned out to pay their respects to the murdered president, whose face had begun to darken from decomposition in its open casket. But Lincoln's journey did not end in everlasting rest. Between 1865 and 1901, his body was moved six times. Indeed, a rumor lingers that his body never made it into his present grave.

Then, the hauntings began. Grace Coolidge, wife of Calvin Coolidge, the thirtieth American president, was reportedly the first person to see the ghost. She came upon him in the Oval Office, gazing sadly out of the windows as the president had often been seen to do in life.

Once, on a state visit, Queen Wilhelmina of the Netherlands answered a knock on the door of the Lincoln Bedroom to find President Lincoln standing there in his top hat. The queen promptly fainted.

Another guest, Winston Churchill, was apparently interrupted by the ghost while he was in the middle of dressing. The unflappable British Prime Minister exclaimed, "You have me at a disadvantage, Sir!" The ghost of Lincoln smiled and obligingly disappeared.

To this day, there is a persistent belief that Abraham Lincoln haunts the White House, and his gravesite in Springfield, Illinois. His funeral train is also said to repeat its ghostly voyage every year on the anniversary of his death.

The Princes in the Tower

Edward V and his brother

With a hollow thud, the shovel that had been slicing through the dirt struck wood. It was an old chest. Excitement sparked between the men, who were making repairs in the Tower of London. The Crown Jewels were housed only a few hundred feet away. What treasure might they have stumbled upon? Holding their breath, they lifted what remained of the lid. Here and there lay scattered shreds of fabric. Then, awakened by their lanterns, they saw a cold and ghastly gleam. It was not the gleam of gold, but of a grinning skull and bones.

ON APRIL 13, 1483, a twelve-year-old boy was proclaimed Edward V, King of England. Although recognized to have a *"ripe understanding, far passing the nature of his youth,"* the new king was still too young to rule. Lucky, then, that he had an uncle to protect him: Richard, Duke of Gloucester.

In May, Edward moved into the Tower of London to await his coronation. Although famous as the site of grizzly executions, the Tower was also a royal palace. Edward was given a luxurious suite of rooms. But within weeks, he would experience the Tower at its most sinister.

On June 12, Richard had one of Edward's most powerful supporters killed and all the king's attendants removed. The *"ripe understanding"* of the young king did not fail him. His doctor reported that Edward, *"like a victim prepared for sacrifice…believed death was facing him."*

Edward's younger brother soon arrived to share his fate. Meanwhile, their uncle declared himself king. From the moment of Richard III's coronation, the two young princes were never seen again—unless you count the many sightings of their ghosts wandering the Tower hand in hand.

Then, almost two hundred years later, workmen fixing a staircase in the Tower discovered a wooden chest buried beneath it. Inside were the skeletons of two children. Could these have been the Princes in the Tower? King Charles II thought so. He gave them a proper burial. Since then, there have been no more sightings of the poor murdered brothers.

Richard III

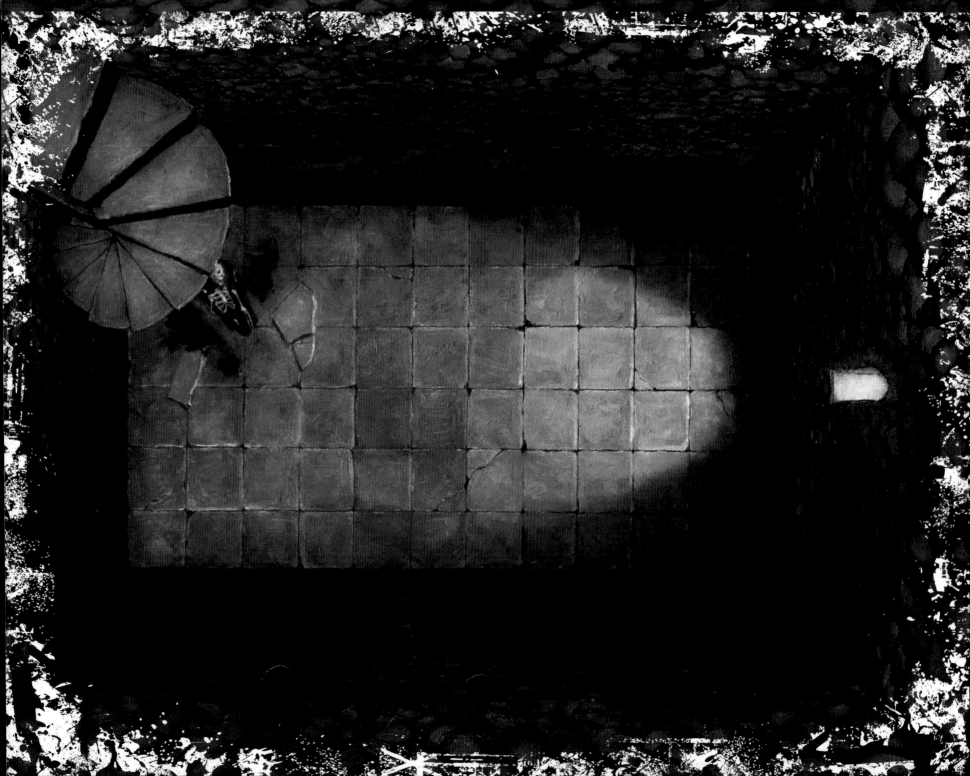

Whalley Abbey

Just before midnight the clouds parted and the light of the full moon washed down, tinting the scene with silver and throwing dark shadows into the corners of the ruins. For one moment all was still and silent. Then a low hum was heard— a noise that soon swelled into a harmony of human voices. One by one, the monks in their deeply hooded habits stepped through the ancient arched doorway. The sight of this brotherhood deep in prayer would have been serene, even comforting, if it wasn't for the fact that the moonlight passed right through them, dancing through their ghostly forms to gleam on the cold stones below.

John Paslew

FROM THE LAYING of its foundation stone in 1308, Whalley Abbey in Lancashire, England, and its community of monks prospered. By Tudor times, Whalley Abbey was known for its wealth—which might have made it a prime target for King Henry VIII's "Dissolution of the Monasteries."

Henry's goal was to take the wealth of the Catholic Church for himself. Not surprisingly, his plan was met with a rebellion, known as "The Pilgrimage of Grace." The monks of Whalley at first refused to take part, but the Pilgrims laid siege to the Abbey. Whalley's abbot, John Paslew, was forced to swear loyalty to the leader of the Pilgrims.

When the rebellion fell apart, Abbot Paslew tried to bribe his way back into the king's good graces. He granted the king's powerful secretary, Thomas Cromwell, a generous pension of ten marks a year from abbey funds. But this did not help. Within ten weeks, *"There was neither Abbot nor Abbey of Whalley."*

The poor abbot was convicted of treason and hanged. The monks of Whalley were thrown out of their home, leaderless and penniless. Some escaped to France. But many, it was said, *"Lingered near the scenes of their former enjoyments, hovering like departed hopes around the ruin to which they clung."* And so they have been seen to linger to this very day, walking and singing in procession behind their doomed leader.

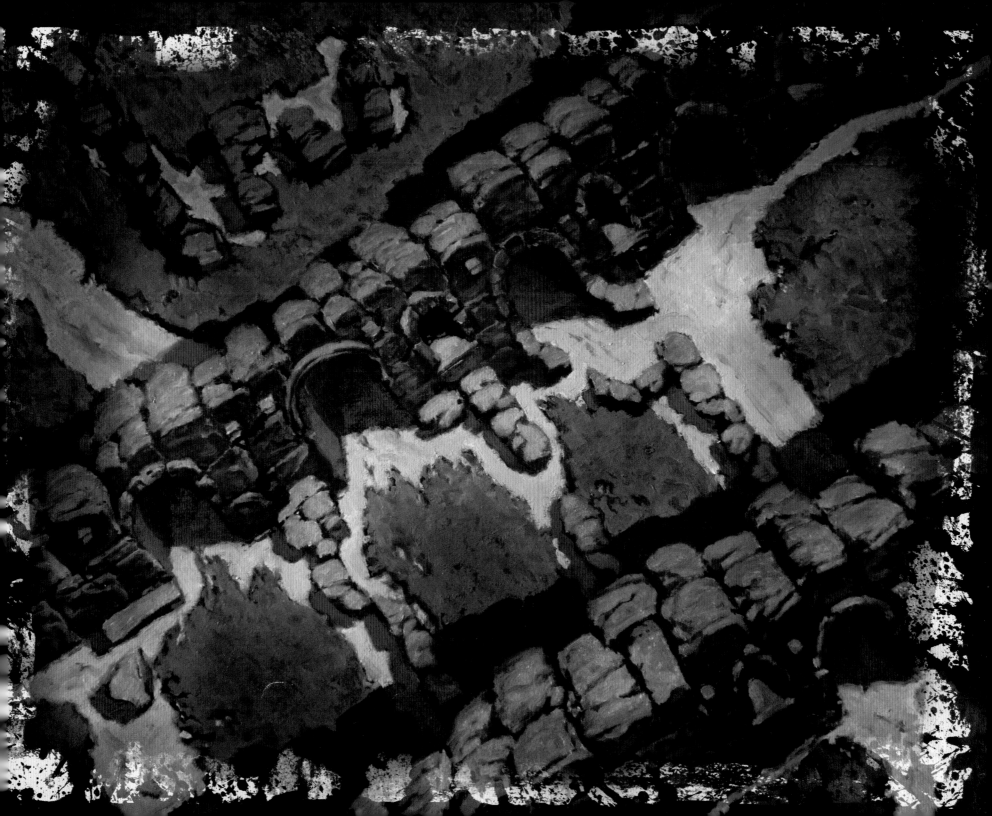

The Brown Lady

Through a narrow gap in the door he watched the figure steadily approaching. She carried a candle. The darkness seemed to part and close around her to the rhythmic swish of her skirts. As she drew level with him, she stopped. Turning, she grinned at him through his spy hole, raising her candle to light the hollows that should have been her eyes.

THE BROWN LADY of Raynham Hall (home of the Marquesses of Townshend in England), is one of history's most famous hauntings. This is due in part to the credibility of its witnesses, which included King George IV before he became king; Colonel Loftus, who even sketched the ghost; and the novelist Captain Frederick Marryat, whose original purpose had been to disprove the haunting. Instead, Marryat had an experience so shocking, recalls his daughter, *"My father never again attempted to interfere with the Brown Lady…"*

Accompanied by two of Lord Townshend's nephews, Marryat hid himself late one night when he saw a light coming down a corridor. The three men had watched as a woman drew closer, until, from her old-fashioned brown dress, they'd recognized her as the infamous ghost. Just then she stopped. Raising her lamp, she grinned at them in such a *"diabolical manner"* that Marryat jumped out from his hiding place and shot her with his pistol at point-blank range. Of course, the Brown Lady immediately disappeared.

In almost every sighting, the ghost is dressed in a brown outfit matching that of an unidentified portrait. Some witnesses also report that, appallingly, the Brown Lady has no eyes. Instead they describe dark hollows, like sockets in a skull. But, in its most famous sighting, the ghost was not wearing brown.

In 1936, a professional photographer, Indra Shira, was asked to capture Raynham Hall's grand staircase. His assistant, Captain Provand, was setting up the camera. Suddenly, Shira saw a spectral figure floating down the stairs. He shouted to Provand to take a picture. Provand could not see what Shira was shouting about, but released the shutter anyway.

What do *you* see on the staircase? Many believe this to be the first ghost ever captured on film.

The Headless Horseman

You're hurrying along a track of muddied leaves elbowing its way through the woods. Just as you'd feared, the sun drops below the horizon. The black-trunked beeches suddenly loom menacing. A rising mist begins to fill the air with wraiths. You sense you're being watched. You stop, heart pounding. And then you realize, that pounding is not your heart. With a drum of hooves and a blast that rips leaves off the trees, a great steed passes you. His rider reins him in. The horse turns, rearing. You stare up at the horseman, numb with terror. He has no head. Or that's what you think until your eyes are dragged by an awful sound to the crook of his arm — and the head cradled there laughing at you.

THE HEADLESS HORSEMAN has charged through the folklore and nightmares of many cultures. In Ireland, the headless Dullaghan rides an enormous black stallion, his phosphorescent head held before him to light his way. His path is marked by the withering of crops and the souring of milk.

In Northern India, the dreaded Dund is still believed to be at large. He rides with his severed head tied before him on the pommel of his saddle, and calls to people in their homes. Entire towns and villages will close their shutters on the rumor that he is near, because hearing his call means death.

In England, there's a legend surrounding High Fernley Hall. In the eighteenth century, it was home to two brothers who loved the same woman. She eventually chose one, and the other committed suicide—

by cutting off his head. He returned every night as a headless horseman to haunt his family, including the unhappy bride.

But arguably, the most famous Headless Horseman is found in Washington Irving's *The Legend of Sleepy Hollow*. In an unforgettable scene, the schoolmaster Ichabod Crane is chased by the ghost of a Hessian trooper who had lost his head to a cannon ball. As Ichabod crosses a bridge to what he thinks is safety, he looks back to see the Horseman hurling his head at him. The Horseman has good aim and his gruesome missile dislodges Ichabod from his horse. The next day, there's nothing to be found of Ichabod. Beside his fallen hat lie the shattered remains of a pumpkin.

The Haunted Gallery

Katherine Howard

After the echoes of the tourists recede, the long hall of Hampton Court Palace settles into an expectant silence. The rising moon throws silver squares through the window panes. Somewhere, a clock ticks. Then, with the rustle of silk, she appears. Hurrying. Anguished. Her arms push aside unseen bodies, stretch desperately toward safety. "Henry!" she cries, "My lord, my lord!"—and almost makes it to his door. But there, an invisible force pulls her back. Despair twists her last words into a wailing shriek. The apparition vanishes. And just as they had in life, her cries fall on deaf ears.

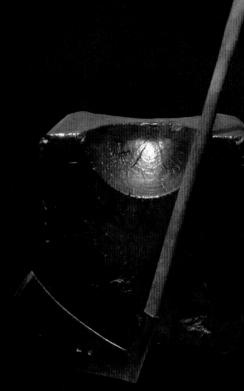

ON JULY 28, 1540, King Henry VIII married for the fifth time. His bride, Lady Katherine Howard, was a petite brunette, graceful and good-natured, and only fifteen years old. She was also the cousin of Henry's second wife, Anne Boleyn, whom he had beheaded for adultery.

If Katherine was repulsed by the aging Henry, who was grossly overweight and covered with pus-filled ulcers, she showed no sign of it. Indeed, Katherine seemed quite delighted with her new life of jewels, dresses, and dancing.

And if her cousin's brutal end gave her cause for caution, Katherine showed no sign of that either. She gave an ex-lover a job as her private secretary and began seeing another lover in secret.

The king was blissfully unaware of his queen's scandalous activities. He was so grateful to have finally found this "rose without a thorn" that he ordered a public thanksgiving to be said. But, to the king's great humiliation, it was at this service that he first learned of Katherine's behavior, through a letter left by his chair.

The queen was immediately confined to her apartments—but guessing that she was facing death, she managed to break free. Caught by guards just before she could reach Henry in his chapel, she was dragged screaming back to her rooms. Katherine would never see the king again.

Katherine entered the Tower of London by the Traitor's Gate, as had Anne Boleyn. She asked for the block to be brought to her room so she could practice placing her head on it. On Monday, February 13, 1542, Katherine, like her cousin, was beheaded. In Katherine's case though, the king did not grant the mercy of the sword. Her head was struck off with an axe. She was only seventeen.

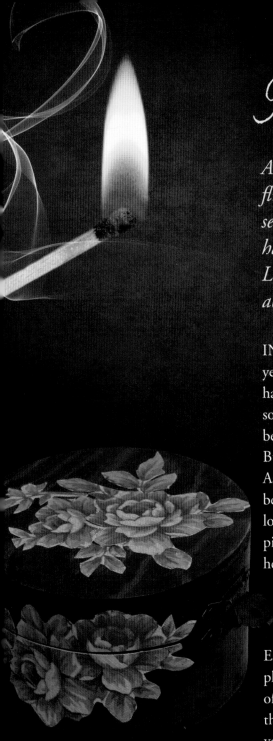

The Amherst Poltergeist

At last she was sleeping. Her hair and lashes were damp. The sedative he'd administered flushed her cheeks. Now, he could think about what he'd seen—the pillows and sheets that seemed to hurl themselves at him with no help from the terrified girl. But surely she must have managed this by some sleight of hand? The sound of scratching interrupted his thoughts. Looking up, he gripped his chair in fright as foot-high letters etched themselves across the wall above the unconscious girl's head...ESTHER COX YOU ARE MINE TO KILL.

IN 1878, in the Canadian town of Amherst, nineteen-year-old Esther Cox found herself at the center of a haunting. It started with a couple of odd events—something stirring inside her mattress, which could have been a mouse, and a box that rose by itself into the air. But one night, Esther's body suddenly started to swell. As she screamed in pain, her skin turned bright red and became hot to the touch. Then, just as abruptly, four loud explosions rang out and Esther fell back against her pillows, her swelling gone, but in such a deep sleep that her family thought she was dead.

Four days later, the mysterious swelling began again. This time, the family summoned the local physician, Dr. Carritte, who proceeded to sedate Esther for *"nervous excitement."* But the strange phenomena continued. Carritte himself witnessed one of the most chilling incidents of all: letters carving themselves into the wall, spelling out "Esther Cox, you are mine to kill."

An exorcism was attempted—during which a pail of cold water began to boil in Esther's presence—but was unsuccessful. Then, lighted matches began materializing in midair, setting fire to parts of the house. Rather than risk getting her family evicted from their rented cottage, Esther left home.

She found work on a farm, but when the barn caught fire, she was sent to jail for arson. Supporters argued that the fire had been set by the poltergeist and poor Esther was released early. Dr. Carritte wrote, *"Honestly skeptical persons were on all occasions soon convinced that there was no fraud or deception in this case...I am certain I could not have believed such apparent miracles had I not witnessed them."* After this, the poltergeist finally left Esther alone.

Black Dogs

As the moon broke free from the clouds, a fiendish howl filled the air. It sucked the life from the open spaces around him and drained the blood from his head. Frozen, he strained to hear where it had come from—in which direction were the echoes receding? But now, all he could hear was the rush of the wind over the moors. It was just a dog, he told himself. And as if summoned by the thought, indeed, a dog stood before him. Black as night. Enormous—by a trick of the light or his fear, as big as a calf or a lion. It's only a dog, he told himself. But then why were its eyes glowing red?

THE BLACK DOGS, the Whisht Hounds, Black Shuck, Old Shuck, or Hell Beast: known by a variety of names and roaming in packs or alone, Black Dogs have haunted England for hundreds of years. Some say that they came with the Vikings. Others claim that they are an incarnation of the Devil. The legends surrounding the dogs vary from county to county, but two beliefs are almost universal: the supernatural nature of the dogs can be seen in their eyes—yellow, green, or red; and the sight of these dogs is an omen of death.

In 1577, at the height of a storm, a Black Dog appeared in Bungay Church in Norfolk. It caused great terror, leaving two worshippers dead, *"strangled at their prayre,"* and another *"as shrunken as a piece of leather scorched in a hot fire."*

Since then, there have been frequent sightings. Black Dogs have been reported loping along country roads and through churchyards, or roaming forests and baying in packs over the moors.

In a relatively recent case, on April 19, 1972, a Royal Coastguard officer, Graham Grant, spotted a Black Dog on Yarmouth Beach in East Anglia. He watched it through his binoculars for a couple of minutes, until it faded away before his eyes. He continued to scan the beach for the next hour, but it never reappeared. He told a fellow officer, Harold Cox, about what he had seen. Cox warned him about the curse, but Grant was not frightened. Ten weeks later, in the chair from which he'd recounted his sighting of the Black Dog, Grant died of a heart attack.

Bloody Mary

Mary Tudor

The giggling died away when the door closed. The girls huddled closer together behind her. On the far wall, the mirror winked at them in the candle light. "Go on," a voice prodded her. "Yes, go on!" She felt herself propelled forward by bony fingers poking her back. It's just a mirror, she thought. The candles flared as if in answer, mocking. Her knees locked. "Do it!" they hissed. "You said you would do it!" I don't have to do anything I don't want, she told herself, a pulse jumping in her throat. She looked at her own frightened features in the cavernous space in the mirror. "I'm not doing this!" she decided out loud. But her face in the mirror remained still and the room was silent. "Stop!" she tried to shout. Her own face looked back at her, unmoved. In the mirror, her lips began to part, forming the words "Bloody Mary…"

UNLIKE THE OTHER HAUNTINGS in this collection, Bloody Mary is not a historical ghost but an urban myth—or, more accurately, a ritual to summon a ghost in a mirror by repeating a phrase. Most commonly, the phrase is "Bloody Mary," to be repeated three, seven, or thirteen times. Sometimes, the name to be chanted is "Mary Worth," or "Mary Whales." In some variations, the sinister taunt "I've killed your baby" is added.

Nobody knows who these Marys are. They do not seem to be related to the English queen, Mary Tudor, who was called Bloody Mary for burning Protestants during her reign. They are sometimes said to be women who have murdered their children, or women who have been murdered themselves, or witches who have been burned or drowned. But the rumors are never very specific.

What happens after Mary is summoned also varies greatly. In some legends, she will kill you. In others, she will scratch and mutilate you or drag you into the mirror, never to be seen again.

Only a few parts of the myth remain consistent: the room in which the mirror hangs must be dark; the mirror must be lit by candles; and the summoner must be prepared to not survive to tell the tale.

Bibliography

Brunvand, Jan Harold. *American Folklore: An Encyclopedia.* Routledge, 1998.

Challoner, Richard. *Modern British Martyrology; Commencing with the Reformation.* Keating, Brown & Co., 1836.

Clayton, John A. *The Lancashire Witch Conspiracy: A History of Pendle Forest and the Pendle Witch Trials.* Barrowford Press, 2007.

Cohen, Daniel. *The Encyclopedia of Ghosts.* Dodd, Mead & Company, Inc., 1984.

Crooke, William. *The Popular Religion and Folk-Lore of Northern India.* Archibald Constable & Co, 1896.

Curran, Bob. *Mysterious Celtic Mythology in American Folklore.* Pelican Publishing Company, Inc., 2010.

Dundes, Alan. *Bloody Mary in the Mirror: Essays in Psychoanalytic Folkloristics.* University Press of Mississippi, 2002.

Guiley, Rosemary Ellen. *The Encyclopedia of Ghosts and Spirits, Second Edition.* Checkmark Books, 2000.

Irving, Washington. *The Legend of Sleepy Hollow and Other Tales.* The Reader's Digest Association, Inc., 1987.

Marryat, Florence. *There is No Death.* Cosimo Classics, 2004.

Matthews, Rupert. *Ghosts and Spirits.* QEB Publishing, Inc., 2010.

Ogden, Tom. *The Complete Idiot's Guide to Ghosts & Hauntings.* Macmillan USA, Inc., 1999.

The Editors of Time-Life Books. *Hauntings.* Time Life Books Inc., 1997.

The Folklore Society (Great Britain). *Folklore, Vol. XIII.* David Nutt, 1902.

Wales, Prince George of. *The Cruise of Her Majesty's Ship "Bacchante".* Macmillan and Co., 1886.

Weir, Alison. *The Princes in the Tower.* Ballantine Books, 1994.

Weir, Alison. *The Six Wives of Henry VIII.* Grove Weidenfeld, 1992.